Preface

Welcome to the comprehensive guide for the " Java EE 7 Application Developer 1Z0 900". This book has been meticulously crafted to serve as your indispensable companion on the journey to achieving mastery in Java Enterprise Edition (Java EE) application development. As technology evolves, the demand for skilled Java developers continues to grow, and this certification is a testament to your expertise in leveraging the robust features of Java EE 7 for building scalable and enterprise-grade applications. Whether you are a seasoned Java developer seeking to validate and enhance your skills or a newcomer aspiring to venture into the dynamic world of enterprise application development, this guide is designed to cater to your needs.

Inside these pages, you will find a comprehensive coverage of the exam syllabus, delving into key Java EE 7 technologies such as Servlets, Java Server Pages (JSP), Java Persistence API (JPA), Contexts and Dependency Injection (CDI), Enterprise JavaBeans (EJB), Java Message Service (JMS), and more. Each chapter is crafted to provide not only theoretical knowledge but also practical insights, hands-on examples, and best practices derived from real-world scenarios. Whether you are aiming to pass the certification exam or looking to deepen your understanding of Java EE 7 application development, this book aims to be your go-to resource.

Furthermore, this guide is designed to be accessible for developers at various skill levels. If you are new to Java EE or transitioning from a previous version, you'll find introductory chapters that set the foundation for more advanced topics. For experienced developers, the book offers in-depth insights, advanced techniques, and guidance on best practices to refine your skills.

AF516752

Table of Contents

“Java EE 7 Application Developer Certification Program”

The "Java EE 7 Application Developer Certification Program" was a certification offered by Oracle for Java developers specializing in enterprise-level application development using Java EE 7 technologies. This certification was designed to validate the skills and knowledge of developers working on Java EE applications, covering various aspects of Java EE architecture, APIs, and best practices.

Key aspects of the Java EE 7 Application Developer Certification Program typically included:

1. Exam Coverage:

The certification program often required candidates to pass one or more exams that covered Java EE 7 technologies, including Servlets, JSP, JPA (Java Persistence API), CDI (Contexts and Dependency Injection), EJB (Enterprise JavaBeans), JMS (Java Message Service), and others.

2. Prerequisites:

Candidates were generally expected to have a solid understanding of Java programming and a background in enterprise application development.

3. Preparation Resources:

Oracle typically provided official study guides, training courses, and other resources to help candidates prepare for the certification exams.

4. Hands-On Experience:

Practical experience with Java EE 7 technologies and hands-on development skills were crucial for success in the certification program.

5. Certification Benefits:

Achieving certification demonstrated a developer's proficiency in Java EE 7 and could enhance career prospects by showcasing expertise in enterprise application development.

6. Renewal Requirements:

Certifications often required periodic renewal to ensure that certified professionals stayed current with the evolving Java EE technologies.

It's important to note that the certification landscape may evolve, and new versions or changes to existing certifications may occur. Therefore, for the most up-to-date and accurate information, it is recommended to check Oracle's official certification website or contact Oracle directly for details on the Java EE 7 Application Developer Certification Program.

Java EE 7 Application Developer Practice Questions Part 1

1. You need to develop a chat application, which allows the display of emoticons and images together with text messages. How should you configure a WebSocket endpoints to receive both text and binary messages?

   A. Create two @onMessage methods in the same endpoint with appropriate parameter types.

   B. Define the @onMessage methods in your endpoint with Object as parameter and check the actual type in our code.

   C. You can achieve this only by creating separate WebSocket endpoints for each message type.

   D. Create two @onMessage methods, each with appropriate decoder attribute in the same endpoint.

   Answer: A

2. Reorder quantities for an item sub inventory are calculated using Fixed Lot Multiple and Round Order Quantity. Assume that the reorder quantity is 24 and you specify 10 for the fixed lot multiple and enable rounding the reorder quantity. What will be the reorder quantity?

   A. 20

   B. 24

   C.30

   D. 25

   Answer: C

3. Which two capabilities are provided by the Java Authentication and Authorization Services (JAAS) API? (Choose two.)

   A. protecting data from unauthorized viewing by using encryption

   B. verifying that a user is allowed to perform an action

   C.ensuring that data is not modified in transit

   D. verifying identity claims from users

   Answer: B, D

4. Which interface should you implement if you want to be alerted to the lifecycle events surrounding your task being executed by a ManagedExecutorService?

   A. the Runnable Interface

   B. the ManagedExecutorTask interface

   C. the TaskEventListener interface

   D. the ManagedTaskListener interface

   Answer: D

5. Given the code fragment:

```
@Path ("Employees")
public class EmployeesResource
        @InjectprivaceEmployeeManagerem;
        @Get
@Path("id:[A-Z] [0-9]+}")
public Employee getEmployee(@PathParam("id") String id) {
        returnem.fmdEmployee(id);
  )
}
```

Which URL triggers the invocation of the getEmployee () method?

A. <base url>/Employees/89724

B. <base url>/Employees/J6349

C. <base url>/Employees/id:a7280

D. <base url>/Employees/id/J6349

Answer: B

6. What is true about Message-Driven Beans (MDBs)?

A. MDBs can participate in transactions.

B. MDBs are invoked synchronously.

C. Each MDBs can process messages only from a single client.

D. MDBs retain data caches between client calls.

Answer: A

7. While performing the task "Create Chart of Accounts, Ledger, Legal Entities, and Business Units in Spreadsheet Task", you mentioned that the legal entity country is the United States of America. What will be the functional currency of the ledger you are defining?

   A. The system will pock the first available currency from the list of Values.

   B. The system will automatically pick "USD" as functional currency from the legal entity country.

   C. It is mandatory to provide functional currency, because ledger cannot be defined without functional currency. The system will throw an error upon processing.

   D. The system will ask the user to provide functional currency at the time of uploading the spreadsheet if it is not provided in the first place.

   E. It is mandatory to provide functional currency because ledger cannot be defined without functional currency. The system will throw an error upon upload of the spreadsheet because all required fields are not populated.

   Answer: B

8. A user is performing a material return transaction against access stock in an Inventory organization ; however, the user fails to select the Physical Material Return Required check box. What happens?

   A. Stock is reserved.

   B. Shipment lines are created.

   C. A transfer order line remains open.

   D. It is considered as accounting-only return.

   Answer: D

9. You have been asked to implement internationalization in your JSF web application. Where do you configure the supported locales?

   A. in the <f:view> tag of the Facelet page

   B. in the web.xml file

   C. in the faces-config.xml file

   D. in the src folder

   Answer: C

10. Given the code fragment:

```
@ReguestScoped
publicclass BankActivityService {
        public void notifyDebit(BankEvent be) { }
        public void notifyCredit(BankEvent be) { }
}
```

Which code can be added to register both of these methods to receive BankEvent notifications only if an instance of BankActivityService is already instantiated in the current context?

A. @Observes(notifyObserver=IF_EXISTS) on line 3 and line 6

B. @Observes(during=IN_PROGRESS) on line 1

C. @Observes(during=AFTER_COMPLETION) on line 1

D. @Observes(notifyObserver=IF_EXISTS) on line 4 and line 7 before method parameter declaration

Answer: A

11. Which code snippet prints the exception error message as part of the page output?

A. <%= exception.message %>

B. <c:out value="${requestScope["˜javax.servlet.error.exception']}"/>

C. <% exception.getMessage(); %>

D. <% System.out.println(e.getMessage()) %>

Answer: D

12. Java EE's support for WS-Security includes handling which two types of security credentials? (Choose two.)

A. X.509 certificates

B. SAML tokens

C. OAuth Bearer tokens

D. Two-factor authentication tokens

Answer: A, B

13. Given the code fragment from a Facelet page:

```
<ui:compositionxmlns="http://www.w3.org/1999/xhtml"
        xmlns:h="http://xmlns.jcp.org/jsf/html"
        xmlns:pt="http://xmlns.jcp.org/jsf/passthrough"
        xmlns:f="http://xmlns.jcp.org/jsf/core'
        xmlns:jsf="http://xmlns.jcp.org/jsff
        xmlns:ui=t'http://java.sun.com/jsf/facelets">
        <h:form id= "searchForm">
                <!--Line 1-->
                <h:commandButton value= "Search"
        </h:form>
</ui:composition>
```

On Line 1, you ae asked to insert a search box that displays the text"Search Here" via a placeholder.Assume searchMB is a valid Managed Bean.Which two options enable you to create a search box with a placeholderattribute on Line 1? (Choose two.)

A. <h:inputText value="#(searchMB.query)"><f:param name="placeholder" value="Search Here"/></h:inputText>

B. <h:inputText value="#(searchMB.query)" placeholder="Search

C. <input jsf:id="search" placeholder="Search here" jsf:value="# (searchMB.query)"></input>

D. <h:inputTextpt:placeholder="Search Here" value="# (searchMB.query)"/>

E. <input id="search" jsf:placeholder="Search Here" value="$(searchMB.query)"></input>

Answer: C, E

14. Your customer wants you to restrict the values of Receivables Transaction Type for their three business units. You created three reference data sets for each business unit. However, the user is still able to see the values in the Transaction Type list of values which are not defined in the business unit data set. What is the reason for this behavior?

A. Reference Data Sets cannot be used uniquely across business units. They can only be used at the Legal Entity level.

B. The user has multiple Business Unit Roles and, therefore, is able to see additional values.

C. Receivables Transaction Types are common across business units.

D. The user is seeing the values defined in the common set. The values should be removed from the common set.

Answer: D

15. Given the code fragment:

```
JAXBContextjc — JAXBContext.newInstance( "com.oracle.foo" );
Unmarshaller u — jc.createUnmarshaller();
InputStream in = new FileInputStream("fooStuff.xml");
Object o — u.unmarshal( in );
```

Which method should be used on line 3 to enable default validationmechanism?

A. u.setProperty(String, Object)

B. u.setProperty(Schema)

C. u.setEventHandler(ValidationEventHandler)

D. u.setAdapter(XmlAdapter)

Answer: D

16. How do you specify a default error page in your web.xml file?

A. <on-error><location>/general-error.html<location></on-error>

B. <error-page><error-code>*</error-code><location>/general-error.html</location> </error-page>

C. <on-error><error-code>*</error-code><location>/general-error.html</location></on-error>

D. <error-page><location>/general-error.html</location></error-page>

Answer: B

17. Given the code fragment:

Account.java:

```
public class Account {
        privateintaccld = 12345;
        / / getters and setters
}
```

Customer.java:

```
public class Customer {
        private Account acc; / /line 1
        public void setAcc(Account acc) / / line 2
        { this.acc=acc; )
        public Account getAcc() / / line 3
        { returnacc; )
```

And –

index. xhtml:

```
<h:outputText value — t' The Id is # (customer. acc.accld)"/>
```

Which two steps, when performed independently, enable the index.xhtml page to print the following text: The Id is 12345? (Choose two.)

A. Replace line 2 with: @Inject public void setAcc(Account acc)

B. Replace line 3 with: @Inject public Account getAcc()

C. Replace line 1 with: @Inject private Account acc;

D. Replace line 3 with: public @Inject Account getAcc()

E. Replace line 1 with: private @Inject Account acc;

F. Replace line 2 with: public void setAcc(@Inject Account acc)

Answer: D, F

18. Given:

```
public class SomeC1ass {
        @Resource (name="java:comp/env/concurrent/TaskExecutor")
        ManagedExecutorServicemes;
        public void createTask() {
                Future<Integer> result=
                        mes.sibmit(new MyCallable<Integer>());
        }
}
```

How often does the submitted task run?

A. need more details to determine

B. once

C. as many times as you like

D. based on a schedule

Answer: A

19. Which three statements are true for an expense destination transfers that does NOT require a receipt at destination inventory organization?

A. The destination inventory is not incremented.

B. There is no put away transaction in Inventory since the item is expensed.

C. There is no cost associated to the transaction.

D. A receipt is required on interorganization expense destination transfer orders between the from and to organizations.

E. The transfer order is considered received and delivered at the time of shipment.

Answer: A, B, C

20. Given:

```
// line 1
public class Mymapper {
@PrePassivate
public void setPinDrop() {}
@PostActivate
public void checkLocation() {}
}
```

What code needs to be added to line 1 for MyMapper bean instances to be correctly passivated?

A. @Stateless @PassivationCapable

B. @Stateless

C. @Stateful @PassivationCapable

D. @Stateful

Answer: D

21. Which URL represents an invalid approach to pass a parameter to a REST resource?

A. <base-url>/Employees?value=1

B. <base-url>/Employees&value=1

C. <base-url>/Employees/1

D. <base-url>/Employees;value=1

Answer: D

22. Given:

```
public class AppException extends Exception {}
    @Stateless
    public class CustomerService {
        @TransactionAttribute(TransactionAttributeType.REQUIRED)
        publicbooleanaddCustomer(int id, String name throws AppException {
        // assume database insert operation succeeds
        Customer c = insertIntoDB(id, name);
        if(id < 20) {
            throw new AppException();
        }
      }
    }
```

If an exception is thrown inside the if block, what effect will it have on the transaction?

A. The transaction will be committed.

B. The transaction will be suspended.

C. The transaction will be rolled back.

Answer: C

23. Given the code fragments:

```
@Stateless
public class HRService {
        @PersistenceContext(unitXame—"HRApp-PU")
        private Employee findEmployee(String badgeld) {
                returnentityManager.find(Employee.c l ass, badgeld);
                }
                public void updateEmployee(Employee emp) {
                / / add code here
                }
    }
    @WebServ l et(name="HR", /hr"))
public class HRServlet extends HttpServlet {
            @EJB
        privateHRServicehrService;
        public void doGet(HttpServ l etRequest req, HttpServletResponse res)
                                        throwsServletException, IOException {
                    String badgeld = req.getParameter("badge");
                String name = req.getParameter("name")
                Employee emp = hrService.findEmployee(badgeld)
                emp.setXame(name);
                hrService.updateEmployee(emp);
            }
    }
```

What code should you add to the body of the updateEmployeemethod in order to save pending changes to the database?

A. entityManager.merge(emp);

B. Context. Ctx = new InitialContext(); UserTransactionutx
= (UserTransaction)ctx.lookup("java:comp/UserTransaction");

utx.begin(); entityManager.merge(emp); utx.commit();

C. entityManager.lock(emp); EntityManager.merge(emp);

D. entityManager.getTransaction().begin();

entityManager.merge(emp);entityManager.getTransaction().commit();

Answer: B

24. When handling a JSF request, your application code decided to redirect the call to another URL by using HTTP redirect. Which action should you take to correctly complete the handling of the JSF life cycle?

A. Set the immediate="true" attribute on the command button that was used to perform this call.

B. Invoke the dispatch() method on the ExternalContext object.

C. Invoke the setCurrentPhaseld(RENDER_RESPONSE) method on the FacesContext object.

D. Invoke the responseComplete() method on the FacesContext object.

Answer: C

25. Given the code fragment:

```
<servlet-mapping>
        / servlet-name>
        <url-pattem>/*</url-pattem>
< / servlet-mapping>
<servlet-mapping>
        <serv1et-name>secondServlet</ servlet-name>
        </url-pattem></url-pattem>
</ servlet-mapping>
<servlet-mapping>
        <servlet-name>thirdServ1et</ servlet-name>
<url-pattem>/</url-pattem>
< / servlet-mapping>
```

When the context root is requested http://host:port/context, how does the container resolve this mapping?

A. thirdServlet handles the request.

B. firstServlet handles the request.

C. The container throws an error at startup.

D. secondServlet handles the request.

Answer: C

26. Given the code fragments:

```
/ / line 1
    public class ContactId implements Serializable {
            private String countryCode;
            private String phoneNumber;
            //remaining implementation
        }
    @Entity
    / / line 2
    public class Contact implements Serializable {
            @notNull
            @Id
            protected String countryCode;
            @NotNull
            @Id
            protected String phoneNumber;
            // remaining implementation
      }
```

Which action completes this composite primary key implementation?

A. Add @IdClass annotation at line 1.

B. Add @Embeddable annotation at line 1 and replace both @Id annotations with @EmbeddedId annotations.

C. Add @IdClass(ContactId.class) annotation at line 2.

D. Add @Embeddable annotation at line 1 and @EmbeddedId(ContactId.class) at line 2.

Answer: D

27. Given the code fragment:

```
// line 1
public class DataConverter
        implementsAttributeConverter<LocalDate, Date> {
        / / implementation
}
@Entity
// line 2
public class Customer {
```

```
        // line 3
        privatelocalDate birthday;
        //remaining implementation
    }
```

How can you apply DateConverter to the birthday field?

A. by adding @Convert(to=Date.class) at line 3

B. by invoking the setConverter(DateConverter.class) method on the EntityManager object

C. by adding @Converter(autoApply=true) at line 1

D. by adding @Convert((DateConverter.class)) at line 2

Answer: A

27. Which class do you use to handle an incoming JSON Message as a stream?

A. JsonReader

B. JsonObjectBuilder

C. JsonParser

D. JsonObject

Answer: A

28. Which two approaches would result in the current date being added to the output of a JSP? (Choose two.)

A. <%= out.println(new java.util.Date()) %>

B. <% out.println(new java.util.Date()); %>

C. <%= new java.util.Date() %>

D. <% System.out.println(new java.util.Date()); %>

Answer: A, C

29. Given the code fragment:

```
@Resource(lookup = "java:comp/Defau1tJMSConnectionFactory")
privateConnectionFactorycf;
CResource(lookup = "jms/MyTopic")
private Topic topic;
public void action() {
        try (JMSContextctx =
                cf.createContext(JMSContext.SESSION_TRANSACTED);){
        JMSConsumer cl — ctx.createConsumer(topic, "(grade > 50)");
        JMSConsumer c2 — ctx.createConsumer(topic, "(grade 50)");
        }
```

}

How are transactions managed?

A. through a single shared transaction across the connection factory

B. through a separate transaction per JMS Consumer

C. through a single transaction for the entire JMS Topic

D. through a single shared transaction in the JMS Context

Answer: D

30. You need to exchange large binary messages using chunks in a WebSocket application. Identify two ways in which you can receive partial messages. (Choose two.)

A. Define an @OnMessage method with a single MimePart parameter.

B. Use a ChunkListener interface implementation.

C. Use a MessageHandler.Partial<ByteBuffer> interface implementation.

D. Define an @OnMessage method with byte [] as the first parameter and a boolean as the second parameter.

Answer: C, D

31. Given:

```
URI uri = new URI("ws:/ / www.example.com/api/employee");
WebSocketContainer container = ContainerProvider.getWebSocketContainer();
Session session= container.connectToServer(new SocketHandler(), uri);
RemoteEndpoint.Async remote = session.getAsyncRemote();
Employee employee = new Employee ("Nancy Taube");
employee. setStatus(Status .FULLTIME);
/ / send employee object
session.close(new CloseReason(CloseReason.CloseCodes.NORMAL_CLOSURE, "Goodbye");
```

Which client-side Java method will send the employee object to the WebSocket Server Endpoint?

A. session.post(employee);

B. container.send(employee);

C. session.send(employee);

D. remote.sendObject(employee);

Answer: A

32. You are working with JMS publish-subscribe operations.What happens when a producer publishes a message to a topic for which a durable subscription exists but there are no subscribers available?

A. The publisher waits for a subscriber, who then consumes it. However, the publisher will time out if no consumer arrives within the given timeout period.

B. The publisher sends the message. However, it is never consumed because there wasn't anything listening when it arrived, regardless of the message timeout length.

C. The publisher successfully sends a message, which will be consumed later, once there is a subscriber, assuming the message hasn't timed out.

D. The message publisher is immediately notified about the lack of subscribers and can decide for itself if, and when, to resend.

Answer: C

33. Which type allows you to share servlet attributes across your entire web application?

A. ServletContext

B. HttpSession

C. ServletRequest

D. ServletConfig

Answer: A

34. Which annotation allows a request to be executed with another Principal's identity?

A. It is not possible to execute a request with another Principal's identity.

B. @UseIdentity

C. @RolesAllowed

D. @Runs

Answer: C

35. Which statement is true about the WS-Security standard?

A. It is a Java EE standard for protecting SOAP services.

B. It relies on HTTP security mechanism to protect SOAP messages in transmit.

C. It provides message-level security.

D. It defines protocol-specific ways of protecting SOAP messages.

Answer: C

36. Which three types of jurisdictions should be considered while designing the Enterprise Structure?

A. Labor Jurisdiction

B. Local Jurisdiction

C. Obligatory Jurisdiction

D. Identifying Jurisdiction

E. Transaction Tax Jurisdiction

F. Income Tax Jurisdiction

Answer: D, E, F

37. Which two statements are true about the relationship between JavaServer Pages (JSP) and servlets? (Choose two.)

   A. A JSP page must extend the HTTPServlet class to behave like a servlet.

   B. A JSP page has access to the same information, objects, and a context as a servlet.

   C. A JSP page is interpreted by JSPServlet.

   D. A JSP page must be written as either an XML file or a JSP file before it is turned into a servlet.

   Answer: A, D

38. Given:

```
@Stateless
public class AlarmManager {
        @Resource
        privateTimerServicetimerService;
        public void createAlarm(Date alarmDate) {
                Alarm myAlarm = new Alarm();
                TimerConfigconfig = new TimerConfig();
                config. setlnfo(myAlarm.getld());
        }
        @Timeout
        public void handleTimeout(Timer myTimer) {
                intalarmld = {int)myTimer.hetlnfo();
                showAlarmMessage(alarmld);
        }
}
```

   You are creating an Alarm management system. When you create a new alarm, you want it to create an alert that is triggered once at the specified time.

   Which method should you call on Line 9 to create the timer?

   A. timerService.createCalendarTimer(alarmDate, config);

   B. timerService.createSingleActionTimer(alarmDate, config);

   C. timerService.createlntervalTimer(alarmDate, -l, config);

   D. timerService.createTimer(alarmDate, -l, config);

   Answer: D

39. Given the code sample:

   public interface GenericMessenger (

   public void handleMessage(Message msg) { }

```
)
And:
@Default
public class MsgHandler implements GenericMessenger (
public void handleMessage(Message msg) { }
)
And:
@Alternative
public class SmsHand1er implements GenericMessenger (
public void handleMessage(Message msg) { }
)
And:
<alternatives>
<c1ass>com.acme.SmsHand1er</c1ass>
< / alternatives>
And this injection point:
@Inject GenericMessengermessageHandler;
```

Which type would be injected at run time and referenced by the messageHandler variable?

A. SmsHandler

B. MsgHandler

C. None of the above. An exception would be thrown due to ambiguous bean references.

D. GenericMessenger

Answer: D

40. On your JSF page, you have a form in which you have a command button:

```
<h:commandButton value="C1ick Me!"
          actionListener=" # {someBean.1istenCarefu1 1y) "
          action="#{someBean.actNow)"/>
```

A user submits the form by clicking the button, and no errors occur while processing the request. Which statement is true?

A. The actNow() and ListenCarefully() methods are executed in parallel.

B. The listenCarefully() method is executed followed by the actNow() method.

C. The actNow() method controls the condition upon which the listenCarefully() method is allowed to be executed.

D. The actNow method is executed followed by the listenCarefully() method.

Answer: B

41. Your customer wants to prevent customer shipments out of a specific subventory. They aresetting up a material status to control this.Which transaction do they need to disallow?

A. Move Request Putaway.

B. Sales Order Issue

C. Miscellaneous Issue

D. Sales Order Pick

E. Ship Confirm

Answer: B

42. Given the code fragment:

```
public void onMessage(Message msg) {
try {
/ / get property names
} catch (Exception e) {
}
```

How can you get all property names of a JMS message in the JMS consumer onMessage operation?

A. String [] props = msg.getPropertyNames();

B. Enumeration props = msg.getPropertyNames();

C. Iterator props = msg.getPropertyNames();

D. List<String> props = msg.getProperties();

Answer: A

43. Given a JSL document describing a batch job:

```
<job id="ProductLoadJob"
xmlns=http://xmlns.jcp.org/xml/ns/javaee version= “1.0”>
<step id="ProcessProduct">
        <chunk item-count= “10”>
                <reader ref="ProductReader"/>
                <processor ref = “ProductProcessor” / >
                <writer ref="ProductWriter"/>
        </chunk>
< / step>
</job>
```

How do you initiate a batch job?

A. Get the JobExecution object from BatchRuntime and call its start() method.

B. Get the JobExecution object from BatchRuntime and set its status to JobStatus.INITIATED.

C. Get the JobOperator object from BatchRuntime and call its start() method.

D. Call BatchRunTime.initialize("ProductLoadJob");

Answer: A

44. You face a supply request exception due to some reason. You realize that you need to make somechanges to the Manage Supply Request Exceptions page.Which action will you perform?

A. The supply request can be updated using a third-party application only.

B. The supply request cannot be updated. The only way is to resolve the error in the source application and resubmit the request.

C. Update the supply request and make sure errors are resolved before resubmitting it.

D. Update the supply request and submit it. The errors will be resolved automatically.

Answer: B

45. Given the code fragment:

```
Cookie cookie = new Cookie ("key","value");
kie.setMaxAge (-1);
```

How long does this cookie persist?

A. until server shutdown

B. until garbage collection in the servlet instance

C. this request

D. until browser shutdown

Answer: D

46. When should a JPA entity implement the Serializable interface?

A. when JPA entities are used in the EJB Full container

B. when JPA entities are used outside of the EJB Lite container

C. always, because JPA entities are required to implement the Serializable interface

D. when JPA entities are used as parameters or return values by the remote EJB operations

Answer: D

47. Which statement is true about JAX-RS resource implementation?

A. The REST resource implementation class must extend the javax.ws.rs.core.Application class

B. The REST resource class can be implemented as a stateful Enterprise JavaBean (EJB).

C. The REST resource class can be implemented as a Plain Old Java Object (POJO).

D. The REST resource implementation class must not be final.

Answer: A

48. Your customer has two warehouses (Inventory organizations) located in two different regions. They have a consigned agreement in place with the supplier. Your customer requests that whenever consumption advice is created, it should be created separately for each inventoryorganization.What setup is required to achieve this requirement?

A. Set Consumption Advice Summary in Consignment Agreement to "All Organizations"

B. Set Consumption Advice Summary in Consignment Agreement to "Organization'.

C. This cannot be achieved because only one common consumption advice is created regardless of other parameters.

D. Set Consumption Advice Summary in Consignment Agreement to "All Organizations withitems".

Answer: B

49. How can you inject a target web service into an EJB?

A. Define service as an injectable resource by using the <resource-ref> declaration.

B. Use a HandlerChain.

C. Use a java.xml.ws.WebServiceRef annotation.

D. Use a java.xml.ws.WebServiceContext annotation.

Answer: A

50. How can you configure, in a portable way, the number of threads used by a ManagedExecutorService?

A. programmatically, using a ManagedExecutorService

B. using the ManagedExecutors utility class to define the execution properties

C. This cannot be done because this configuration is dependent on the Java EE Product Provider.

D. configuring the thread pool info in the deployment descriptor

Answer: A

Java EE 7 Application Developer Practice Questions Part 2

51. Given an HttpServletRequest request and an EJB SessionContextctx.Which is a valid way to retrieve the Principal invoking either behavior?

    A. request.getCallerPrincipal() and ctx.getCallerPrincipal()

    B. request.getUserPrincipal() and ctx.getUserPrincipal()

    C. request.getCallerPrincipal() and ctx.getUserPrincipal()

    D. request.getUserPrincipal() and ctx.getCallerPrincipal()

Answer: A

52. Your customer is a very large organization spanning across multiple countries. Their legal requirements, Human Resource Policies, and Functional Currencies for Ledger are different foreach country. Your customer wants to maintain 10 different companies in the system.Which combination meets this requirement?

    A. 10 Enterprises, 1 Division, where each division has 10 legal entities and 1 ledger

    B. 1 Enterprise, 10 Divisions, where each division has its own ledger with common legal entity across all divisions

    C. 10 Enterprises, 10 Divisions, where each division has its own legal entity and ledger

    D. 1 Enterprise, 10 Divisions, where each division has its own legal entity and ledger

Answer: D

53. Given the set of navigation rules:

```
<navigation-rule>
<from-view-id>list-widgets</ from-view-id>
        <navigation-case>
                <from-outcome>add</from-outcome>
                <to-view-id>add-widget</to-view-id>
        </navigation-case>
<navigation-rule>
        <from-view-id>*</from-view-id>
        <navigation-case>
                <from-outcome>home</ from-outcome>
                <to-view-id>home</to-view-id>
        </navigation-case>
        <navigation-case>
                <from-outcome>logout</ from-outcome>
                < to-view-id>goodbye</to-view-id>
```

```
</navigation-rule>
</navigation-rule>
        <from-view-id>home</from-view-id>
        <navigation-case>
                <from-outcome> dashboard< / from-outcome>
                <to-view-id>dashboard</to-view-id>
        </navigation-case>
        <navigation-case>
                < from-outcome> list< from-outcome>
                <to-view-id>list-widgets<</to-view-id>
</navigation-rule>
```

Which two define a valid flow of view IDs through the application? (Choose two.)

A. home > goodbye > list-widgets

B. dashboard > home > add-widget> list-widgets

C. list-widgets > add-widget > home > dashboard > home

D. home > list-widgets > add-widget > goodbye

Answer: C, D

54. How can a servlet indicate to the browser that cookie data should be sent over a secure connection?

A. Call the getSecure(true) method on the cookie object.

B. Encrypt the cookie data. The browser automatically sends encrypted data over a secure connection.

C. Set the ENCRYPT header in the response.

D. Configure SessionTrackingMode.SSL on the ServletContext object.

Answer: A

55. Your company has multiple inventory organizations where goods are transferred internally. A user has created a new organization but new organization is unavailable when creating an inter organization transfer.What is the missing setup?

A. The destination organization transfer type is In Transit.

B. Interorganization Parameters are not set up between the organizations.

C. Inventory organization data access for users is not set up.

D. The source and destination organization doesn't belong to the same legal entity.

Answer: D

56. You defined an Inventory Organization that is meant to track the contract manufacturing process outsourced to a supplier. Where do you mention that this

Inventory Organization is meant for one particular supplier?

A. Manage Item Organizations

B. Manage Inventory Organizations

C. Manage Subinventories

D. Manage Contract Manufacturing Relationships

E. Manage Inventory Organization Locations

Answer: B

57. The Applications Development Framework Desktop Integration (ADFdi) user interface is supported in Oracle Fusion Receiving, Inventory Management, and Shipping products.Identify four ADFdi user interfaces that are supported.

A. Manage Lot/Serial Interface

B. Upload ASN or ASBN

C. Review Count Interface Records

D. Manage Shipment Message Interface

E. Manage Inventory Transaction Correction in Spreadsheet

F. Review Receipts Interface

Answer: A, D, E, F

58. Which two features are provided by the JSTL Core library for a JSP? (Choose two.)

A. iteration over a collection

B. buffering of large result sets

C. testing conditions

D. message localization

Answer: A, D

59. You need to load on-hand balances for go live. Which template should be used for this?

A. InventoryReservationImportTemplate.xlsm

B. InventoryMiscellaneousTrxTemplate.xlsm

C. InventoryTransactionImportTemplate.xlsm

D. InventoryOnHandBalanceTemplate.xlsm

E. InventoryBalanceImportTemplate.xlsm

Answer: C

60. Which three applications originate a buy request that is received by supply chain orchestration?

A. Accounts Payable

B. Purchasing

C. Inventory

D. Self Service Procurement

E. Planning

F. Order Management

Answer: C, E, F

61. Your customer wants to transfer material from facility A to facility B.They are using the interorganization transfer to perform the transaction in the system. The requirement is "whenever material is transferred from their facility A to facility B, facility B needs to pay 5% additional amount to the current item cost".Which task must be set up to accomplish this requirement?

A. Manage Cost Plus Pricing

B. Manage Transfer Pricing Rules

C. Manage InterorganizationMarkup

D. Manage Organization Relationships

E. Manage Cost Organization Relationships

Answer: E

62. Which of these can be a JPA entity?

A. Enum type

B. Abstract class

C. Interface type

D. Final class

Answer: A

63. Your client has just up their chart of accounts. They are now designing the organization hierarchy in the system. Which three structures should the customer use the to do this?

A. Warehouse, Subinventory, and Locators

B. Divisions, Business Units, and Departments

C. Cost Centers, Organizations, and Locations

D. Cost type, Default Cost Structure, and Item Organization

Answer: B

64. You created two filters for your web application by using the @WebFilter annotation, one for authorization and the other for narrowing results by the provided search criteria. The authorization filter must be invoked first. How can you specify this?

A. setting the priority attribute of the @WebFilter annotation for each of the filters

B. placing the filter mapping elements in the required order in the web.xml deployment descriptor

C. placing @WebFilterMapping annotations in the required order

D. specifying the filter precedence order by using the @Priority annotation

Answer: A

65. Identify two valid WebSocket message types for which you can register handlers. (Choose two.)

A. Error Message

B. Binary Message

C. Pong Message

D. Ping Message

Answer: B, C

66. Which two elements CANNOT be injected by using an @Inject annotation? (Choose two.)

A. static fields

B. instance fields declared final

C. concrete methods

D. abstract methods

Answer: B, D

67. For an Item to be enabled for back-to-back order process, which attribute do you need to set?

A. Item attribute: Reservations Enabled

B. Organization attribute: Allow Reservations

C. Item attribute: Back-To-Back Enabled

D. Item attribute: Allow purchase orders off of sales orders

E. Organization attribute: Allow Back to Back Processing

Answer: C

68. Given the following code:

```
@WebServlet(urlPatterns = {"/myServ1et), asyncSupported=true}
public class NonblockingServlet extends HttpServlet{
protected void processRequest (HttpServletRequestreq,
                                    HttpServletResponse res)
                            throwsServletException, IOException {
        AsyncContext ac = req.startAsync();
```

```
            // line 1
        }
    }
```

What should you do at line 1 to enable this servlet receive request data without blocking?

A. Use a Runnable instance with the start () method of AsyncContext.

B. Define a ReadListener and assign it to the request input stream.

C. Create a Callable class and delegate this operation to a ManagedExecutorService by using the dispatch method of AsyncContext.

D. Define an AsyncListener and assign it to the AsyncContext object.

Answer: D

69. An inventory transaction is important to the system through an FBDI template.Which transaction state denotes that an inventory transaction is created in the Oracle InventoryManagement application?

A. Validated

B. Created

C. Staged

D. New

E. Deferred

Answer: A

70. Your client has decided that Discrete Manufacturing will be implemented at a future stage, so any new supply from current manufacturing will be added to current inventory by the Open Transactions Interface. The immediate requirement is to go live with Inventory and OrderManagement.Which two seeded transaction types can be omitted for material status control?

A. All Transaction Types Related to Work in Process

B. Average Cost Update

C. All Internal Transactions

D. Backflush Subinventory Transfer

E. Miscellaneous Issues and Receipts

Answer: A, D

71. As part of implementing Oracle Cloud for your customer, you defined multiple Business Units. The customer wants you to define an Inventory Organization that is associated with all the business units and not just one particular business unit. How do you achieve this?

A. It is not possible to define an Inventory Organization that is associated with more than one business unit.

B. Leave the Management Business Unit field blank in the Inventory Organization definition.

C. Leave the Profit Center Business Unit field blank in the Inventory Organization definition.

D. Define the Inventory Organization without associating it with any location.

Answer: A

72. Your organization is planning for a periodic counting of individual items automatically throughout the course of the year. As part of this activity, the user has loaded items to the cycle count but some of the items are not being considered when count schedules and count sequences are notgenerated.Identify two reasons that explain why the items are not being considered.

A. The Cycle Count Enabled flag is not selected for the inventory organization.

B. The Cycle Count Enabled flag is not selected for the item.

C. The Include in Schedule option is not selected to include the item for auto-scheduling.

D. The approval controls are not set up.

E. The ABC assignment group is not defined.

Answer: B, D

73. Your organization performs a restock via a transfer order between inventory organizations, using the following parameters for processing:

-Transfer Type: In-transit transfer type

-Receipt Routing: Standard

-Transfer Order Required: Yes

During the process, the receiving organization wants to make a change to the transfer order line.After which fulfillment stage will they no longer be able to change the transfer order?

A. Awaiting Fulfillment

B. Awaiting Receiving

C. Ship Confirm

D. Closed

E. Awaiting Billing

Answer: D

74. You are in the process of analyzing the demand and supply schedules for the item based on high level reservations.

A. Account Alias

B. Work Order

C. Transfer Order

D. On Hand

E. Requisition

F. Movement Request

Answer. C

75. Which is a valid description of REST?

A. REST provides the same architectural properties as SOAP.

B. REST is a library that is part of JEE called JAX-RS.

C. REST is the conventional way of interacting with information resources.

D. REST is a Web Services standard supported by JEE and JAX-RS.

Answer: D

76. Given the code fragment:

```
public class Bean {
}
@SessionScoped
public class Service {
        @Inject
        private Bean bean;
}
```

Assuming this bean is used only in the code fragment above, how long will the injected Bean instance be available?

A. for the lifetime of the enterprise application

B. for the lifetime of the request

C. for the lifetime of the session

D. for the lifetime of the Service object

Answer: D

77. You have a high value item that you want to audit on an unscheduled basis to deter pilfering. Which method would you use to do this?

A. Automated Cycle Count

B. Blind Inventory Count

C. ABC Count

D. Physical Inventory Count

E. Manual Cycle Count

Answer: E

78. You want to allow one set of roles to POST to a resource and another set of roles to GET it. Which two configuration options should you use? (Choose two.)

A. two separate @HttpMethodConstraints annotations and sets of roles

B. a single @HttpMethodContstraint annotation and a map of method to roles

C. two <web-resource-collection> with different <http-method> in the deployment descriptor

D. a single <web-resource-collection> with two <auth-constraint> with different <http-method> in the deployment descriptor

Answer: B, D

79. Your class requires multiple resources defined, as shown in the following:

```
@<XXXX>({
        @Resource(name="aFactory",
                type="javax.jms.ConnectionFactory"),
        @Resource(name="aSession",
                type="javax.mail.Session">
})
```

You have a set up min-max planning at the subinventory level with the following to source itemAS12312 for Organization: MI:

-Source Type: Organization

-Organization: MI

What type of supply request will be generated?

A. Purchase Requisition

B. None; this is an invalid setup

C. Intra organization transfer order

D. Internal Requisition

E. Movement request

Answer: C

80. Which annotation do you use to group multiple @Resource declarations together for class-based injection, replacing <XXXX> in the code above?

A. @Resources

B. @Resource

C. @ResourceGroup

D. @ResourceCollection

Answer: B

81. A Persistence application locks entity x with a LockModeType.PESSIMISTIC_READ lock type. Which statement is true?

A. LockModeType.PESSIMISTIC_READ is the synonym of LockModeType.READ

B. This operation will force serialization among transactions attempting to read the entity data.

C. This operation will result in a TransactionRolledbackException if the lock cannot be obtained.

D. If the application updates the entity later, and the changes are flushed to the database, the lock will be converted to an exclusive look.

Answer: B

82. You are building the User Preferences page of an application. A user can change values, such as his or her name, password, address, company, and so on.These values are sent to a CDI backing bean via AJAX when the user tabs out of each field. However, the values must be retained in the CDI bean and stored in the database only when the user clicks the Save button. Which two scopes will allow your CDI bean to retain its state while the user is interacting with the User Preferences page? (Choose two.)

A. Dependent

B. View

C. Session

D. Request

E. Application

Answer: C, D

83. Given:

```
@Path("Employees")
public class EmployeesResource {
        @Inject
        privateEmployeeManagerem;
        @GET
        public List<Employee>findAll() {
                returnem.findAll Employees();
         }
}
```

What will be the response to a HEAD request?

A. The findAll() method will be called and the employee list will be returned.

B. The findAll() method will be called and no employees will be returned.

C. No method will be invoked and no error will be returned.

D. No method will be invoked and a 404 error will be returned.

Answer: C

84. Your web application requires logic to remember items that a user placed into a shopping cart. Which two mechanisms should you use to associate that information with the user? (Choose two.)

A. HttpServletResponse objects

B. ServletContext objects

C. HttpSession objects

D. a database

Answer: B, C

85. Which code snippet indicates that the page you are designing is capable of handling errors?

A. <%@page errorPage= “errorHandler.jsp”%>

B. <%= requestScope["˜javax.servlet.error'] !=null %>

C. <%@page isErrorPage="true"%>

D. <c:setvar="errorHandler" value="true"/>

Answer: C

86. A Java EE application that uses an EJB container must communicate with a legacy system developed using non-Java technologies. Which two Java EE technologies can be used in the integration tier of the application? (Choose two.)

A. JMS

B. JSF

C. JPA

D. JCA

Answer: A, B

87. Which statement is true about the relationship between HTTP and WebSockets?

A. A WebSocket connection is a bi-directional HTTP session with message-handling support.

B. A WebSocket connection is initialized with an HTTP handshake.

C. AWebSocket connection can be initialized by either client or server.

D. A WebSocket connection uses HTTP protocol to exchange data with the browser.

Answer: D

88. What are two outcomes when a lot expires on an item with lot control enabled?

A. It cannot be reserved for a date beyond the expiration date.

B. It remains an inventory, but is not considered on-hand when the user is performing min-maxor reorder point planning calculations.

C. It cannot be transacted.

D. It is issued out of stores.

E. It is not included in cycle counts.

Answer: A, B

89. Given

```
@Singleton
public class MySessionBean {
    / / line 1
public void callMethod() {
    //implementation logic
    }
    / / Constructor and other business methods
}
```

Which annotation do you use on line 1 to ensure that clients immediately time out when attempting to concurrently invoke callMethod () while another client is already accessing the bean?

A. @AccessTimeout (value = 1, unit = TimeUnit.SECONDS)

B. @AccessTimeout (null)

C. @AccessTimeout (-1)

D. @AccessTimeout (0)

Answer: D

Java EE 7 Application Developer Practice Questions Part 3

90. Which statement is true about Java methods that are exposed as Web Service operations by using JAX-WS API?

    A. The @WebResult annotation must exist.

    B. Method parameters and return types must be JAXB compatible.

    C. Method parameters must be declared by using @WebParam.

    D. The @WebMethod annotation must exist.

Answer: D

91. Given the code fragment:

```
protected void service(HttpServletRequestreq, HttpServletResponse res)
                throwsSenletException, IOException {
PrintWriter out = res.getWriter();
out.print("Service() method called.");
protected void doGet(HttpServletRequestreq, HttpServletResponse res)
                throwsServletException, IOException {
PrintWriter out = res.getWriter();
Out.print("Get()method called.");
```

What output will be returned when this servlet is called a GET request?

    A. Service() method called.

    B. Service() method called.Get() method called.

    C. An HTTP error

    D. GET() method called.

Answer: A

92. Given the JPQL code fragment:

Select pub.title, pub.author, pub.pages FROM Publisher pub

Which two clauses do you add to this JPQL query to retrieve only those books with between 500 and 750 total ages? (Choose two.)

    A. WHERE MIN(pages) >= 500 AND MAX(pages) <= 750

    B. WHERE pub.pages<= 500 OR pub.pages>= 750

    C. WHERE pub.pages BETWEEN 500 AND 750

    D. WHERE pub.pages<= 500 AND pub.pages>=750

Answer: A, B

93. Give the code fragment:

```
@Stateless
public class Warehouse {
public void sendConfirmation(String msg) { }
public String reverve(Product pro) { }
}
```

And the code fragment:

```
@Stateless
public class Shop {
    @EJB private Warehouse war;
public void purchase(Product pro) {
        String confirmationCode = war.resene(pro);
war. sendConfirmation(confirmationCode);
  }
}
```

The sendConfirmation() and reserve() methods should be executed in the same transactional context.

Which transaction attributes do you ensure this?

A. Add annotations: @TransactionAttribute (TransactionAttributeType.REQUIRES_NEW) at line 2, @Transactional at line 9 and @TransactionAttribute ((TransactionAttributeType.MANDATORY) at line 12

B. No additional annotations are required.

C. Add annotations: @TransactionAttribute (TransactionAttributeType.REQUIRED) at line 2, @Transactional at line 9 and @TransactionAttribute ((TransactionAttributeType.REQUIRES_NEW) at line 12

D. Add annotations: @TransactionAttribute (TransactionAttributeType.MANDATORY) at line 2, @Transactional at line 9 and @TransactionAttribute ((TransactionAttributeType.REQUIRES_NEW) at line 12

Answer: D

94. Your supplier sent you stock against a consigned agreement. You transferred at the stock to owned and generated a consumption advice. An invoice was raised by the supplier and the payment made. A few days after using some of the quantities of the stock, you realized that some of the stock sent by the supplier is not of suitable quality and you need to send the stock back. What is the process of returning the material?

A. You have to cancel the invoice and send the material back without changing the ownership.

B. Return the material and create a debit memo for the supplier.

C. You cannot return consigned items that are invoiced and paid. Treat the material as scrap.

D. You have to transfer the ownership of item and perform the return transaction.

Answer: B

95. Your client wants certain inventory items of high importance to be counted periodically to improve the average level of inventory accuracy. What type of counting would you recommend?

A. Physical Count

B. Manual Count

C. Serialized Count

D. Cycle Count

E. Blind Count

F. Zero Quantity Count

Answer: D

96. A shipment has not yet been created for a pick that you are running.How is the due date calculated?

A. system date

B. earliest acceptable date from the order line

C. promise date from the order line

D. request date from the order line

E. schedule ship date from the order line

Answer: E

97. Given the JPQL code fragment:

Select pub.title, pub.author, pub.pages FROM Publisher pub

Which two clauses do you add to this JPQL query to retrieve only those books with between 500and 750 total pages? (Choose two.)

A. WHERE MIN(pages) 500 AND MAX(pages) <- 750

B. WHERE pub.pages c-- 500 AND pub.pages

C. WHERE pub.pages<- 500 OR pub.pages 750

D. WHERE pub.pages BETWEEN 500 AND 750

Answer: A, C

98. Your organization is using min-max planning to replenish stock and the planning parameters are set at item organization level with a default subinventory.

-Item: A, Min Qty: 25, Max Qty: 150 and Current Level: 20

The item above is purchased from a supplier. Although there is subinventory on hand, the sub inventory is below the minimum required level. This should trigger a Min-Max report entry, but the requisition is not generated. Why?

A. Item is not defined in Manage Item Subinventories.

B. Rounding the Reorder Quantity is disabled.

C. No value has been set for the "Min-Max Replenishment Reorder Approval" profile.

D. Min-Max planning can be performed at the Organization level.

E. Fixed lot multiplier is not set.

Answer: A

99. Which three values are applicable for the profile option - "Transaction Processing Mode" for sub inventory transfer and interorganization transfer?

A. Background Processing

B. Sequential Processing

C. Online Processing

D. Concurrent Processing

E. Offline Processing

F. Blind Processing

Answer: A, C, D

100. You have been assigned to the Widget Editor portion of an application. It contains a Widget EditorFacelet page, the Widget class, and a simple WidgetEditor backing bean, which contains a reference to the current Widget instance.

Given the code fragment from the Widget class:

```
public class Widget implements Serializable {
        private String name;
        private Date createdDate;
        privateboolean approved;
}
```

Given the code fragment from the Facelet page:

```
<h:messages id="messages"/>
```

```
<h:form id="widgetForm">
        <h:outputLabel for="name" value = “Name:”/>
        <h:inputTextid = “name” value="#{widgetEditor.widget.name}"/>
        <h:outputLabel for="createdDate" value= “Created Date:”/>
        <h:inputTextid = “createdDate”
                value="#{widgetEditor.widget.createdDate)"/><- - Line 1 - ->
        <h:outputLabel for =“approved” value = “Approved:”/>
        <h:se1ectBooleanCheckbox id="approved"
                value = “#{widgetEditor.widget.approved}" / >
        <h:commandButton value = “Save” action="#{widgetEditor.save)"/>
</h:form>
```

The page displays Conversion Error when a user fills out all the form fields and clicks the Savebutton.

Which step do you perform to fix this problem?

A. Insert <f:convertDateTime"/> at Line 1

B. Replace Line 1 with:<h: inputText

C. Enclose the code fragment within the <f:view/> tag

D. Replace Line 1 with:<h:inputText id="createDate"value="#{widgetEditor.widget.createdDate}"xf:convertDateTime pattern="dd-mm-yyyy"/>4h:inputText>

Answer: D

101. A third-party service equipment is used for various purposes in a manufacturing facility and needs to be overhauled once a year. This equipment is charged based on its consumption without a project dependency.At this point, it should be transferred out of the vendor's warehouse for maintenance and then returned back in the future depending upon the requirement.The material stock transfer should happen with an offline approval and with an account alias as a logical reference.What is the ideal way to handle this process?

A. Miscellaneous Transaction

B. Subinventory Transfer

C. Transfer Order

D. Move Request

E. Requisitions

Answer: A

102. What three Key Performance Indicators are available in the Warehouse Operations Dashboard?

A. Inventory Value

B. Hit or Miss Accuracy

C. Shipment Value

D. Exact Matches Rate

E. Distributed Value

F. Cycle Count

Answer: A, B, D

103. Identify three statements that are true about reservations in back-to-back processing.

A. Reservation supplies that can be reserved are Purchase Orders, Transfer Orders, WorkOrders, and On Hand inventory.

B. Reservations cannot be created for back-to-back On Hand supply orders.

C. Changes to reservation in Oracle Logistics Cloud leads to exceptions, which are displayed in the Supply Chain Orchestration work area.

D. Partial fulfillment of reservations is supported.

E. One reservation is created for a demand and supply.

Answer: A, C, E

104. Material is transferred between the Sub inventories within an organization via transfer order. The setup is complete and the transfer order is created through the FBDI process.What is the primary interface data that needs to be completed in the template?

A. INV_ SUBINVENTORY_TRANSFER

B. INV_ TRANSACTION_LOTS _INTERFACE

C. INV_ TRANSACTIONS _INTERFACE

D. INV_SERIAL_NUMBERS_INTERFACE

E. CST_I_ INCOMING_TXN_COSTS

Answer: C

105. In the Back-to-Back (82B) Order to Cash flow, ordered items are purchased from a supplier. The Sourcing Rules have been defined for the item and the buy flow has been initiated. The salesorder line is shown as Awaiting Shipping and the supply line status is in "Purchasing" with the supply order generated but the purchase requisition not generating. What is the reason?

A. Supply order is generated with exceptions.

B. The sourcing rule is incorrect.

C. No Blanket Purchase Agreement (BPA) exists for this supplier-item combination.

D. Prepare is not valid.

E. Buy requests originate from Order Management.

Answer: B

106. You are a shop floor manager and you have received an order which is a back-to-back order innature. You need to reserve 100 pieces of an item in order to finish you order. However, there are only 50 pieces available for reservation.If you process this request, how many pieces are provided as the fulfillment for the order?

A. 50 pieces, because full 100 quantities are not available.

B. O pieces, because partial fulfillment of reservation not supported.

C. 25 pieces, only half of the quantities can be reserved.

D. 100 pieces, 50 from on-hand and 50 in the form of a purchase order.

Answer: B

107. While negotiating the terms of the consignment agreement, the buyer and the supplier mutually agree to set aging onset point as receipt and the aging period as five days. The terms also say that the consumption advice will be generated daily. In which three scenarios will the goods be transferred from the supplier's ownership to buyer's ownership?

A. You received the goods today and you transfer the ownership using the "create transfer to owned transaction" task.

B. You received the goods today and you decided to issue the goods after days without transferring the ownership.

C. You received the goods today and for the next one week you do not plan any action on the same.

D. You received the goods today and after three days you transfer the ownership using the"create transfer to consigned transaction" task.

E. You received the goods and after four days you return the material to the supplier.

F. You received the goods today after six days you decide to transfer the ownership using the"create transfer to consigned transaction" task.

Answer: A, B, C

108. You are working with JMS publish-subscribe operations.What happens when a producer publishes a message to a topic for which a durable subscriptionexists but there are no subscribers available?

A. The publisher successfully sends a message, which will be consumed later, once there is a subscriber, assuming the message hasn't timed out.

B. The publisher waits for a subscriber, who then consumes it. However, the publisher will time out if no consumer arrives within the given timeout period.

C. The message publisher is immediately notified about the lack of subscribers and can decidefor itself if, and when, to resend.

D. The publisher sends the message. However, it is never consumed because there wasn't anything listening when it arrived, regardless of the message timeout length.

Answer: A

ONLINE RESOURCES

Online Exam Form link -https://forms.office.com/r/dfPvzKhQdZ

Scan QR Code-

ADDITIONAL RESOURCES

YouTube Video Links-

Introduction of Java-https://youtu.be/D2ixfO5_Jac

OOP's Concept -https://youtu.be/psb5GhfbIMk

Introduction To Microsoft SQL Server- https://youtu.be/ea8J7PsfaEc

DBMS Introduction- https://youtu.be/SwB6RTAQ-o0

Introduction of My SQL -https://youtu.be/-7NOhrJoDko

© Author and Publisher 2024

9 789369 722648

Printed at Repro India Ltd.